Preparing you for your Purpose Partner

(12 STEPS TO PREPARING YOU FOR YOUR PURPOSE PARTNER)

DEDICATION

This book is dedicated to my late father who passed away in 2011 Jerome Middlebrooks.

And my spiritual father Bishop Michael Byrd who passed away in 2024.

These two have impacted my life most and kept me spiritually grounded.

PRAYER FOR PURPOSE PARTNER

Heavenly Father, in the mighty name of Jesus, I come to You seeking a purpose partner. Lord, I turn to You because You know everything about us and what is best for us. Help me to surrender my own desires and embrace Your will in this area of my life. I come to You today seeking your wisdom and direction. I feel a deep desire to find a purpose partner - someone who can walk alongside me and help me discover and fulfill the unique purpose you have for my life.

Please lead me to the right person who can encourage me, challenge me, and inspire me to greater heights. Help us to build a strong spiritual foundation and to support one another in our individual callings. I understand that a purpose partner is a divine connection sent by You, meant to fulfill Your greater plan for my life.

Lord, I am at a point where I only want what You have ordained for me. I am ready to receive all that You have for me, trusting in Your perfect timing and wisdom. Grant us the courage to be vulnerable, the patience to grow together, and the discernment to recognize your hand at work. May our partnership bring glory to your name and further your kingdom here on earth.

Thank You for listening to my heart's cry and for hearing this prayer. In Jesus' name, Amen.

PRAYER FOR DEDICATION OF LIFE TO CHRIST

Dear Lord, I come before you today with an open and willing heart, I desire to dedicate my life to you and your purpose fully

Lord, I confess you are my King and the Creator of all things, and that my life is not mine. Everything I am and everything I have comes from you. I want to live to honor you with the way I live.

I surrender my life to you completely, my hopes, my dreams, my fears, my failures, my success and all, take charge today and forever in Jesus name, Amen.

Table of Contents

DEDICATION i

PRAYER FOR PURPOSE PARTNER ii

PRAYER FOR DEDICATION OF LIFE TO CHRIST iii

INTRODUCTION 1

Relationship with God 2

    Building a Deep Relationship with God: Tapping into His Presence: Matthew 22:37-38 2

        Practical Steps: 3

        Spiritual Reflection: 4

        Closing Thought: 4

Understand God's Vision 5

    Discovering God's Vision: Aligning Your Life and Relationship with His Plan: Psalm 1:2 5

        Practical Steps: 6

        Spiritual Reflection: 7

        Closing Thought: 7

Cultivate Godly Character and Integrity 8

    Building a Foundation of Godly Character and Integrity: Ecclesiastes 7:1 8

        Practical Steps: 9

        Spiritual Reflection: 10

        Closing Thought: 10

Practice Self-Control 11

- Embracing Self-Control: The Path to Spiritual and Relational Strength: 11
  - Practical Steps: 12
  - Spiritual Reflection: 13
  - Closing Thought: 13

Submit to God's Will 14

- Trusting God's Plan: Embracing His Will for Your Life and Relationship: 14
  - Practical Steps: 15
  - Spiritual Reflection: 16
  - Closing Thought: 16

Establish Financial Responsibility and Stewardship 17

- Stewardship and Financial Wisdom: Honoring God with Your Resources: 17
  - Practical Steps: 18
  - Spiritual Reflection: 19
  - Closing Thought: 19

Communicate Openly, Honestly, and Respectfully 20

- The Art of Effective Communication: Building Trust and Understanding 20
  - Practical Steps: 21
  - Spiritual Reflection: 22
  - Closing Thought: 23

Personal Growth and Accountability 24

- Embracing Growth and Accountability: Building a Stronger You: 24
  - Practical Steps: 25

    Spiritual Reflection: 26

    Closing Thought: 27

Resolve Conflicts in a Christ-like Manner 28

  Navigating Conflicts with Grace and Understanding: 28

    Practical Steps: 29

    Spiritual Reflection: 30

    Closing Thought: 31

Know Your Position in the Relationship 32

  Embracing Your Role and Responsibilities in Love: 32

    Practical Steps: 34

    Spiritual Reflection: 35

    Closing Thought: 36

Encourage, Edify, and Build Up Each Other 37

  Strengthening Each Other in Love and Faith: 37

    Practical Steps: 38

    Spiritual Reflection: 40

    Closing Thought: 40

Pursue Holiness and Sexual Purity 41

  Embracing Purity and Holiness in Your Relationship: 41

    Practical Steps: 43

    Spiritual Reflection: 44

    Closing Thought: 44

CONCLUSION..45
    Embracing God's Blueprint for Relationships...45
        Spiritual Reflection: 48

INTRODUCTION

Gen 2 vs 23

And Adam said: "This is now bone of my bones And flesh of my flesh; She shall be called Woman, Because she was taken out of Man."

Love is the genuine revelations of the person of God rooted in God's character, it means to be Selfless, Sacrificial Commitment to another's well-being that reflects Christ's love for the church, it is the pathway that guides relationship towards Christ's purposes.

Proverbs 18:22 (NIV), says, *"He who finds a wife finds what is good and receives favor from the Lord."*

This scripture emphasizes the importance of a Christian or godly partnership by emphasizing that finding a spouse is not just a personal blessing but a divine favor.

To build a relationship that honors God, you must be intentional and have a deep spiritual foundation. Which choice do you need to make? What steps should be taken? Join me as we journey to the opening of our Minds, Soul, Spirit, and Eyes in consideration of certain principles and instructions.

Relationship with God

TAPPING IN WITH GOD

Building a Deep Relationship with God: Tapping into His Presence: Matthew 22:37-38

The foundation of any God-ordained partnership starts with your bond, with God. To truly prepare for your destined partner it's vital to connect with God's presence and nurture a relationship with Him. God teaches us to love, knowing the essence of creation was birth through love, all things bright and beautiful, the stars, seas, firmament, plants, hills, mountains, animals, and Man, even down to rescuing Man from the grasp of sin, that sacrifice, the unconditional love. This connection forms the basis for all relationships, in other words, this means putting God first, that relationship is the cornerstone upon which all other relationships are built.

Your relationship with God impacts every area of your life including how you approach relationships. By focusing on your growth you cultivate qualities such as patience, kindness, and unconditional love which are crucial in a godly partnership. A strong relationship with God helps you discern His will, face life's obstacles or navigate life's challenges, and remain steadfast in your faith.

"Draw near to God, and he will draw near to you." **(James 4:8 ESV)**

God desires a close relationship with you. Spend time in prayer, immerse yourself in His Word, and seek His guidance in every aspect of your life. By drawing closer to God, you open your heart to His wisdom and direction, which will be essential in finding and nurturing a relationship that honors Him.

Consider the story of David, a man after God's own heart (Acts 13:22). Despite his flaws and mistakes, David's deep relationship with God guided him through his life. He sought God's direction in every situation, whether facing Goliath (1 Samuel 17) or seeking forgiveness for his sins (Psalm 51).

David's life demonstrates the importance of aligning oneself with God's will, showing that true strength and guidance come from a close relationship with the Creator.

Practical Steps:

- **Daily Prayer and Meditation:** Set aside time each day to pray and meditate on God's Word. This practice will help you hear His voice more clearly and align your desires with His will.
- **Bible Study:** Engage in regular Bible study to understand God's teachings and how they apply to your life and relationships. Consider joining a study group for deeper insights and community support.
- **Worship:** Incorporate worship into your daily routine. Singing praises, listening to worship music, and attending church services can enhance your spiritual connection.
- **Service:** Serve others in your community. Acts of kindness and service reflect God's love and help you grow spiritually.
- **Reflection:** Take time to reflect on your spiritual journey. Journaling your thoughts and prayers can help you track your growth and recognize God's work in your life.
- **Seek God's Will:** Continually ask God to reveal His plans and purpose for your life. **Proverbs 3:5-6 (NIV)** says, *"Trust in the Lord with all your heart and lean*

not on your own understanding; in all your ways submit to him, and he will make your paths straight."

- **Accountability Partner:** Find a trusted friend or mentor who can help you stay accountable in your spiritual walk. Hebrews 10:24-25 (NIV) reminds us of the importance of encouraging one another and meeting together regularly.
- **Fasting:** Periodically fasting can deepen your spiritual connection by removing distractions and focusing your heart on God. Matthew 6:16-18 (NIV) teaches us about the proper attitude toward fasting.

Spiritual Reflection:

Think about your current relationship with God. Are there areas where you can grow closer to Him? Pray for guidance and strength as you commit to deepening your relationship with Him. Remember, a strong relationship with God will illuminate your path and prepare you for a purposeful partnership.

Closing Thought:

By prioritizing your relationship with God, you lay a solid foundation for a future partnership. When you are deeply connected to God, you become more attuned to His guidance, making it easier to recognize and embrace the purpose partner He has chosen for you. Trust in His timing and plan, knowing that He desires the best for you.

Understand God's Vision

For Your Life and Relationship

Discovering God's Vision: Aligning Your Life and Relationship with His Plan: Psalm 1:2

Understanding God's vision for your life and relationship is crucial in building a partnership that honors Him. When you have a clear sense of God's purpose for your life, you can seek a partner who shares that vision and is committed to walking the same path. This alignment ensures that your relationship is not just based on mutual affection, but also a shared mission and divine purpose.

Embracing God's vision helps you prioritize what truly matters and avoid distractions. It empowers you to make decisions that align with His will, fostering a relationship rooted in faith and purpose. By focusing on His vision, you invite His blessings and guidance, paving the way for a fulfilling and harmonious partnership.

"Where there is no vision, the people perish: but he that keepeth the law, happy is he." **(Proverbs 29:18 KJV)**

God's vision provides direction and purpose. When you understand His vision for your life, you can make decisions that are in line with His will, leading to a fulfilling and purposeful existence. A prime example of this is the story of Abraham. God called Abraham to leave his homeland and go to a land He would show him (Genesis 12:1-3). Abraham's obedience to God's vision not only blessed him but also set the foundation for a great nation.

Consider also the life of Joseph, who had dreams revealing God's plan for his future (Genesis 37:5-10). Despite facing numerous trials, Joseph remained steadfast in his faith, trusting in God's vision. His journey from slavery to becoming a ruler in Egypt illustrates how understanding and aligning with God's vision can lead to extraordinary outcomes, even when the path seems uncertain.

Practical Steps:

- **Prayer for Revelation:** Regularly seek God in prayer to reveal His plans for your life and relationship. **Jeremiah 33:3 (NIV)** says, *"Call to me and I will answer you and tell you great and unsearchable things you do not know."*

- **Study the Scriptures:** Dive into the Bible to understand God's character and promises. Scriptures like Romans 8:28 (NIV) assure us that God works all things together for the good of those who love Him and are called according to His purpose.

- **Seek Wise Counsel:** Surround yourself with spiritually mature mentors and friends who can offer godly advice and encouragement. **Proverbs 15:22 (NIV)** says, *"Plans fail for lack of counsel, but with many advisers they succeed."*

- **Reflect on Your Passions and Gifts:** Consider the talents and passions God has placed in your heart. These can often provide clues about His vision for your life. Ephesians 2:10 (NIV) reminds us that we are created in Christ Jesus to do good works, which God prepared in advance for us to do.

- **Write Down the Vision: Habakkuk 2:2 (NIV)** instructs, *"Write down the revelation and make it plain on tablets so that a herald may run with it."* Documenting God's vision for your life can help you stay focused and committed.

Spiritual Reflection:

Take time to reflect on the vision God has for you. Are there areas in your life where you need to align more closely with His will? Pray for clarity and strength to pursue His vision with dedication and faith.

Closing Thought:

Understanding and embracing God's vision for your life and relationship is foundational to experiencing His best for you. As you seek His guidance and align your actions with His plans, you'll find that your path becomes clearer and more fulfilling. Remember, a relationship built on God's vision is not only strong but also purpose-driven, bringing glory to Him in all you do.

Cultivate Godly Character and Integrity

Building a Foundation of Godly Character and Integrity: Ecclesiastes 7:1

Cultivating godly character and integrity is essential for a strong, healthy relationship. These qualities form the bedrock of trust and respect, which are crucial for any partnership to thrive. Godly character involves reflecting Christ-like attributes such as love, patience, kindness, humility, and honesty in all aspects of your life. Integrity, on the other hand, is about being truthful and consistent in your actions, aligning your behavior with your values and beliefs.

Developing godly character requires intentional effort and a commitment to spiritual growth. This process often involves self-reflection, prayer, and a willingness to allow the Holy Spirit to transform your heart and mind. As you grow in godly character and integrity, you become a reliable and trustworthy partner, capable of building a relationship that honors God and stands the test of time.

"A good name is more desirable than great riches; to be esteemed is better than silver or gold." **(Proverbs 22:1 NIV)**

The Bible emphasizes the importance of godly character and integrity. Daniel is a prime example of a man who demonstrated unwavering integrity. Despite the pressures and challenges he faced, Daniel remained faithful to God and was known for his honesty and uprightness (Daniel 6:4). His commitment to godly principles not only earned him respect but also divine favor and protection.

Another biblical example is Joseph, who maintained his integrity despite being falsely accused and imprisoned (Genesis 39:7-20). His steadfast character and trust in God eventually led to his rise to a position of great authority in Egypt. Joseph's life demonstrates that integrity and godly character can lead to significant blessings and opportunities, even in the face of adversity.

Practical Steps:

- **Daily Devotions and Prayer:** Spend time each day reading the Bible and praying. This helps you stay connected to God and grow in His likeness. **Psalm 119:11 (NIV)** says, *"I have hidden your word in my heart that I might not sin against you."*

- **Practice Honesty and Transparency:** Be truthful in your words and actions. **Ephesians 4:25 (NIV)** encourages us to *"put off falsehood and speak truthfully to your neighbor."*

- **Seek Accountability:** Find a trusted friend or mentor who can hold you accountable and encourage you in your spiritual journey. **Proverbs 27:17 (NIV)** states, *"As iron sharpens iron, so one person sharpens another."*

- **Reflect on Your Actions:** Regularly evaluate your behavior and ask God to reveal any areas where you need to grow. **Psalm 139:23-24 (NIV)** says, *"Search me, God, and know my heart; test me and know my anxious thoughts. See if there is any offensive way in me, and lead me in the way everlasting."*

- **Embrace Humility:** Recognize that cultivating godly character is a lifelong process that requires humility and dependence on God. **Philippians 2:3 (NIV)** urges us to *"do nothing out of selfish ambition or vain conceit. Rather, in humility value others above yourselves."*

Spiritual Reflection:

Consider how your current character and integrity align with God's standards. Are there areas where you need to seek His guidance and strength to improve? Pray for the Holy Spirit to work within you, transforming you to reflect Christ more fully in your relationships.

Closing Thought:

Building a foundation of godly character and integrity is vital for a relationship that honors God. As you commit to growing in these areas, you'll find that your relationships become stronger and more resilient. Remember, a partnership built on trust, honesty, and godly principles will not only bring joy and fulfillment but also glorify God in every aspect.

Practice Self-Control

Embracing Self-Control: The Path to Spiritual and Relational Strength:

Self-control is a crucial virtue in both our spiritual journey and relationships. It involves mastering our desires, emotions, and behaviors to align with God's will and purpose. By practicing self-control, we can make choices that honor God and promote healthy, respectful relationships. Self-control helps us avoid actions driven by impulse or emotion, allowing us to respond thoughtfully and with grace. *"Like a city whose walls are broken through is a person who lacks self-control."* **(Proverbs 25:28 NIV)**.

In relationships, self-control fosters patience, understanding, and a peaceful environment. It prevents conflicts and misunderstandings by encouraging us to think before we speak or act. This virtue is essential in maintaining purity and honoring boundaries within a relationship. Practicing self-control enables us to resist temptations and remain steadfast in our commitment to God's principles.

"But the fruit of the Spirit is love, joy, peace, forbearance, kindness, goodness, faithfulness, gentleness and self-control. Against such things there is no law." **(Galatians 5:22-23 NIV)**. Self-control is a fruit of the Spirit, highlighting its importance in the life of a believer.

Daniel exemplified self-control by refusing to defile himself with the royal food and wine, choosing instead to honor God with his dietary choices (Daniel 1:8). His decision not only demonstrated his commitment to God but also led to favor and wisdom. Another example is Joseph, who showed remarkable self-control when he resisted the advances of Potiphar's wife (Genesis 39:7-12). Despite the temptation and potential consequences, Joseph remained faithful to God and maintained his integrity. His steadfastness ultimately led to his rise to power and fulfillment of God's plan for his life.

Practical Steps:

- **Seek the Holy Spirit's Guidance:** Regularly pray for the Holy Spirit to develop self-control within you. **Galatians 5:16 (NIV)** says, *"So I say, walk by the Spirit, and you will not gratify the desires of the flesh."*
- **Set Clear Boundaries:** Establish and maintain personal boundaries in your relationships. **Proverbs 25:28 (NIV)** warns, *"Like a city whose walls are broken through is a person who lacks self-control."*
- **Practice Mindfulness:** Yeah, mindfulness is putting your heart in a conscious state, that is, being mentally alert. Be mindful of your thoughts and emotions, taking captive any that do not align with God's will. **2 Corinthians 10:5 (NIV)** encourages us to *"take captive every thought to make it obedient to Christ."*
- **Develop Healthy Habits:** Cultivate habits that promote self-discipline, such as regular prayer, Bible study, and fasting. **1 Corinthians 9:25 (NIV)** reminds us, *"Everyone who competes in the games goes into strict training. They do it to get a crown that will not last, but we do it to get a crown that will last forever."*
- **Accountability:** Partner with a trusted friend or mentor who can hold you accountable and provide support. **Ecclesiastes 4:9-10 (NIV)** states, *"Two are better than one... If either of them falls down, one can help the other up."*

Spiritual Reflection:

Reflect on areas in your life where you struggle with self-control. Are there specific triggers or situations that challenge your ability to remain disciplined? Pray for strength and seek practical ways to improve your self-control, trusting that the Holy Spirit will guide and empower you.

Closing Thought:

Practicing self-control is essential for a healthy, God-honoring relationship. As you grow in this virtue, you'll find that your interactions become more loving, patient, and respectful. Self-control not only protects your relationship from unnecessary conflicts but also ensures that your actions reflect your commitment to God and His principles.

Submit to God's Will

Trusting God's Plan: Embracing His Will for Your Life and Relationship:

"Understanding God's Vision for Your Life and Relationship" Submitting to God's will is a foundational principle for living a Christ-centered life and nurturing a God-honoring relationship. It involves trusting that God's plan is perfect and that He knows what is best for us, even when it contradicts our desires. **Proverbs 3:5-6 (NIV)** advises, *"Trust in the Lord with all your heart and lean not on your own understanding; in all your ways submit to him, and he will make your paths straight."* This means letting go of our own agendas and seeking God's direction in every aspect of our lives.

In relationships, submitting to God's will entails seeking His guidance in choosing a partner, making decisions, and resolving conflicts. It requires humility, patience, and faith, as we trust that God's timing and plans are superior to our own. This submission fosters a deeper spiritual connection between partners, as they learn to rely on God together. It also helps ensure that the relationship is rooted in biblical principles, promoting a union that honors God.

"Trust in the Lord with all your heart and lean not on your own understanding; in all your ways submit to him, and he will make your paths straight." **(Proverbs 3:5-6 NIV)**. This emphasizes the importance of relying on God's wisdom rather than our own. Jesus Himself modeled perfect submission to God's will. In the Garden of Gethsemane, He prayed, *"My Father, if it is possible, may this cup be taken from me. Yet not as I will, but as you will."* **(Matthew 26:39 NIV)**. Despite His anguish, Jesus submitted to the Father's plan, ultimately leading to our salvation.

Another example is Mary, the mother of Jesus, who responded to the angel Gabriel with humble submission: *"I am the Lord's servant," Mary answered. "May your word to me be fulfilled."* **(Luke 1:38 NIV)**. Her willingness to submit to God's will brought forth the Savior of the world.

Practical Steps:

- **Pray for Guidance:** Regularly seek God's direction through prayer, asking for clarity and wisdom. **James 1:5 (NIV)** promises, *"If any of you lacks wisdom, you should ask God, who gives generously to all without finding fault, and it will be given to you."*

- **Study the Bible:** Immerse yourself in God's Word to understand His will and align your life with His principles. **Psalm 119:105 (NIV)** says, *"Your word is a lamp for my feet, a light on my path."*

- **Seek Godly Counsel:** Surround yourself with wise, spiritually mature individuals who can offer guidance and support. **Proverbs 11:14 (NIV)** advises, *"For lack of guidance a nation falls, but victory is won through many advisers."*

- **Be Patient and Trusting:** Trust that God's timing and plans are perfect, even when they differ from your own expectations. **Isaiah 55:8-9 (NIV)** reminds us, *"For my thoughts are not your thoughts, neither are your ways my ways,"* declares the Lord.

- **Surrender Your Plans:** Be willing to let go of your desires and embrace God's will, trusting that His plans are for your good. **Jeremiah 29:11 (NIV)** assures, *"For I know the plans I have for you," declares the Lord, "plans to prosper you and not to harm you, plans to give you hope and a future."*

Spiritual Reflection:

Reflect on areas of your life where you may struggle to submit to God's will. Are there desires or plans you need to surrender? Pray for the strength and faith to trust God fully, knowing that His ways are higher and His plans are perfect.

Closing Thought:

Submitting to God's will is a profound act of faith and trust. As you surrender your plans and embrace His guidance, you'll experience a deeper sense of peace and purpose. Remember, God's will is always for your good and His glory, and His plans will lead you to the abundant life He has promised.

Establish Financial Responsibility and Stewardship

Stewardship and Financial Wisdom: Honoring God with Your Resources:

Financial responsibility and stewardship are critical components of a healthy, God-honoring relationship. As stewards of the resources God has entrusted to us, we are called to manage our finances wisely and generously. This involves budgeting, saving, giving, and living within our means. **1 Timothy 6:17 (NIV)** advises, *"Command those who are rich in this present world not to be arrogant nor to put their hope in wealth, which is so uncertain, but to put their hope in God, who richly provides us with everything for our enjoyment."*

In a relationship, financial stewardship fosters trust and unity. Partners must communicate openly about their financial goals, create a budget together, and make decisions that reflect their shared values and priorities. This approach not only ensures financial stability but also aligns the couple's financial practices with biblical principles. By honoring God with their finances, couples can experience greater peace, purpose, and provision in their relationship.

"Honor the Lord with your wealth, with the firstfruits of all your crops; then your barns will be filled to overflowing, and your vats will brim over with new wine." **(Proverbs 3:9-10 NIV)**. Encourages us to honor God with our finances by prioritizing giving and trusting in His provision. It is a reminder that our resources are a gift from God and should be used to glorify Him and bless others.

Consider the example of the widow's offering in **Mark 12:41-44**. Jesus observed the rich giving large amounts, but it was the poor widow who gave two small coins that caught His attention. He said, *"Truly I tell you, this poor widow has put more* *into the treasury than all the others. They all gave out of their wealth; but she, out of her poverty, put in everything—all she had to live on."* This story illustrates that the heart behind our giving matters more to God than the amount. It challenges us to trust God fully and be generous with what we have, no matter how little it may seem.

Practical Steps:

- **Create a Budget:** Establish a budget that aligns with your financial goals and values. **Proverbs 21:5 (NIV)** states, *"The plans of the diligent lead to profit as surely as haste leads to poverty."*

- **Save Wisely:** Set aside a portion of your income for savings to ensure financial stability and preparedness for future needs. **Proverbs 6:6-8 (NIV)** advises, *"Go to the ant, you sluggard; consider its ways and be wise! It has no commander, no overseer or ruler, yet it stores its provisions in summer and gathers its food at harvest."*

- **Give Generously:** Prioritize giving as an act of worship and trust in God's provision. **2 Corinthians 9:7 (NIV)** encourages, *"Each of you should give what you have decided in your heart to give, not reluctantly or under compulsion, for God loves a cheerful giver."*

- **Live Within Your Means:** Avoid debt and live within your financial capacity to maintain peace and avoid unnecessary stress. **Romans 13:8 (NIV)** instructs, *"Let no debt remain outstanding, except the continuing debt to love one another."*

- **Communicate Openly:** Discuss financial matters regularly with your partner to ensure transparency and mutual understanding. **Amos 3:3 (NIV)** asks, *"Do two walk together unless they have agreed to do so?"*

Spiritual Reflection:

Reflect on your current financial practices. Are there areas where you need to improve your stewardship? Pray for wisdom and guidance in managing your resources, and ask God to help you align your financial practices with His will. Meditate on the truth that everything you have is a gift from God, and consider how you can honor Him through your financial decisions.

Closing Thought:

Establishing financial responsibility and stewardship is vital for a strong, God-honoring relationship. As you manage your resources wisely and generously, you not only ensure financial stability but also honor God and reflect His love and provision. Remember, true financial stewardship is about trusting God with your resources and using them to glorify Him and bless others.

Communicate Openly, Honestly, and Respectfully

The Art of Effective Communication: Building Trust and Understanding

Effective communication is the cornerstone of any healthy relationship. It involves expressing thoughts, feelings and needs openly, honestly, and respectfully. In **Ephesians 4:25 (AMP)**, we are reminded, *"Therefore, rejecting all falsehood [whether lying, defrauding, telling half-truths, spreading rumors, any such as these], speak truth each one with his neighbor, for we are all parts of one another [and we are all parts of the body of Christ]."* This emphasizes the importance of truthfulness and integrity in our interactions.

Open communication fosters trust and understanding between partners. It allows for the sharing of joys, concerns, and aspirations, creating a deeper emotional connection. By speaking honestly, couples can address issues before they escalate, ensuring a harmonious and supportive environment. Respectful communication acknowledges the value of each person's perspective, promoting a culture of mutual respect and consideration.

In practical terms, this means listening actively, avoiding assumptions, and speaking with kindness and empathy. **Proverbs 15:1 (AMP)** states, *"A soft and gentle and thoughtful answer turns away wrath, but harsh and painful and careless words stir up anger."* This highlights the power of gentle and considerate communication in maintaining peace and harmony in relationships.

James 1:19-20 (AMP) offers profound wisdom on communication: *"Understand this, my beloved brothers and sisters. Let everyone be quick to hear [be a careful, thoughtful listener], slow to speak [a speaker of carefully chosen words], and slow to anger; for the [resentful, deep-seated] anger of man does not produce the righteousness of God [that standard of behavior which He requires from us]."* Encourages us to prioritize listening over speaking, to be thoughtful in our words, and to manage our emotions.

Consider the relationship between David and Jonathan. Their bond was strengthened by open and honest communication. In **1 Samuel 20:4 (AMP)**, Jonathan said to David, *"Whatever you say, I will do for you."* This willingness to listen and support each other was pivotal in maintaining their trust and friendship, even in challenging times. Their relationship exemplifies the power of transparent and respectful communication in fostering strong, enduring connections.

Practical Steps:

- **Practice Active Listening:** Focus on truly understanding your partner's words and emotions. Reflect back on what you hear to confirm understanding, and avoid interrupting. **Proverbs 18:13 (AMP)** advises, *"He who answers before he hears [the facts]—It is folly and shame to him."*
- **Express Yourself Clearly:** Use "I" statements to convey your feelings and needs without blaming or accusing. For instance, say, "I feel upset when..." instead of "You always..." This approach reduces defensiveness and fosters constructive dialogue.

- **Be Honest and Transparent:** Share your thoughts and feelings honestly, even when it's uncomfortable. **Ephesians 4:15 (AMP)** instructs, *"But speaking the truth in love [in all things—both our speech and our lives expressing His truth], let us grow up in all things into Him [following His example] who is the Head—Christ."*

- **Show Respect and Empathy:** Acknowledge your partner's perspective and show empathy. Respectful communication builds trust and demonstrates love and care. **Colossians 4:6 (AMP)** reminds us, *"Let your speech at all times be gracious and pleasant, seasoned with salt, so that you will know how to answer each one [who questions you]."*

- **Resolve Conflicts Peacefully:** Address conflicts with a focus on resolution and understanding, not winning an argument. Follow the example of Jesus, who taught us to be peacemakers. **Matthew 5:9 (AMP)** says, *"Blessed [spiritually calm with life-joy in God's favor] are the makers and maintainers of peace, for they will [express His character and] be called the sons of God."*

Spiritual Reflection:

Take time to reflect on your communication habits. Are there areas where you need to improve in openness, honesty, or respect? Pray for God's guidance to enhance your communication skills, and meditate on scriptures that emphasize the power of words and the importance of truthful and loving dialogue.

Closing Thought:

Mastering the art of communication is vital for building a strong, God-centered relationship. As you and your partner commit to open, honest, and respectful communication, you will foster deeper trust, understanding, and connection. Remember, effective communication is a continuous journey that requires intentionality and grace.

Personal Growth and Accountability

Embracing Growth and Accountability: Building a Stronger You:

Personal growth and accountability are essential for anyone preparing for a purposeful partnership. Growth involves continuously striving to become a better version of oneself, while accountability means being responsible for one's actions and decisions. As individuals, we are called to continuously develop our character, skills, and faith. This growth is not just for our benefit but also for the enrichment of our relationships. **Proverbs 27:17 (AMP)** states, *"As iron sharpens iron, so one man sharpens [and influences] another [through discussion]."* Emphasizes on the importance of relationships that encourage personal development and mutual improvement, i.e. mutual growth and accountability in fostering strong, healthy relationships.

In a purposeful partnership, both individuals should encourage each other to pursue personal growth and hold one another accountable. Growth is a journey that requires self-awareness, reflection, and a willingness to change. It involves setting goals, seeking knowledge, seeking spiritual and personal development, and being open to feedback. Accountability partners can be vital in this process, offering support, encouragement, and honest feedback. In a relationship, both partners should commit to personal growth and hold each other accountable, fostering a dynamic where both individuals can flourish.

This means taking time for self-reflection, identifying areas for improvement, and making a plan to address them. It also involves seeking accountability through trusted friends, mentors, or spiritual advisors who can provide guidance and support. As partners grow individually, they bring more to the relationship, enhancing its strength and depth.

Hebrews 10:24-25 (AMP) encourages us, *"And let us consider [thoughtfully] how we may encourage one another to love and to do good deeds, not forsaking our meeting together [as believers for worship and instruction], as is the habit of some, but encouraging one another; and all the more [faithfully] as you see the day [of Christ's return] approaching."* This highlights the importance of community and mutual encouragement in personal growth.

Consider the relationship between Paul and Timothy. Paul served as a mentor and accountability partner to Timothy, guiding him in his spiritual journey and encouraging him to grow in his faith. In **1 Timothy 4:12 (AMP)**, Paul writes, *"Let no one look down on [you because of] your youth, but be an example and set a pattern for the believers in speech, in conduct, in love, in faith, and in [moral] purity."* Paul's mentorship helped Timothy develop into a strong leader, demonstrating the impact of accountability and growth in a spiritual context.

Practical Steps:

- **Set Personal Goals:** Identify areas in your life where you want to grow, such as your spiritual life, career, or relationships. Set specific, achievable goals and create a plan to reach them. **Philippians 3:13-14 (AMP)** says, *"Brothers and sisters, I do not consider that I have made it my own yet; but one thing I do: forgetting what lies behind and reaching forward to what lies ahead, I press on toward the goal to win the [heavenly] prize of the upward call of God in Christ Jesus."*

- **Seek Feedback:** Be open to receiving feedback from others. Constructive criticism can provide valuable insights into areas where you can improve. **Proverbs 12:1 (AMP)** reminds us, *"Whoever loves instruction and discipline loves knowledge, but he who hates reproof and correction is stupid."*
- **Find an Accountability Partner:** Choose someone you trust to hold you accountable for your goals. This person should encourage you, provide honest feedback, and pray for your growth. **Ecclesiastes 4:9-10 (AMP)** states, *"Two are better than one because they have a more satisfying return for their labor; for if either of them falls, the one will lift up his companion. But woe to him who is alone when he falls and does not have another to lift him up."*
- **Reflect and Adjust:** Regularly reflect on your progress and make adjustments as needed. Be patient with yourself and remember that growth is a continuous process. **Lamentations 3:40 (AMP)** advises, *"Let us test and examine our ways, and let us return to the Lord."*

Spiritual Reflection:

Take time to reflect on your personal growth journey. Are there areas where you need to improve or seek accountability? Pray for God's guidance and strength to grow in these areas, and meditate on scriptures that encourage personal development and accountability.

Closing Thought:

Embracing personal growth and accountability is vital for building a strong, God-centered relationship. As you commit to growing individually and holding each other accountable, you will create a partnership that is resilient, supportive, and spiritually enriching. Remember, growth is a lifelong journey that requires dedication, humility, and a willingness to learn.

Resolve Conflicts in a Christ-like Manner

Navigating Conflicts with Grace and Understanding:

Conflict is an inevitable part of any relationship, but resolving conflicts in a Christ-like manner is essential for maintaining peace and unity. In **Matthew 18:15-17 (AMP)**, Jesus provides clear guidance on addressing conflicts: *"If your brother sins, go and show him his fault in private; if he listens and pays attention to you, you have won back your brother. But if he does not listen, take along with you one or two others, so that every word may be confirmed by the testimony of two or three witnesses. If he pays no attention to them, refusing to listen and obey, tell it to the church; and if he refuses to listen even to the church, let him be to you as a Gentile and a tax collector."*

Resolving conflicts in a Christ-like manner means approaching disagreements with humility, patience, and a desire for reconciliation. It involves listening to understand rather than to respond, speaking the truth in love, and seeking common ground. By addressing conflicts with grace and understanding, couples can strengthen their relationship and foster a deeper sense of trust and respect.

This implies taking a step back when emotions run high, praying for wisdom and guidance, and approaching your partner with a heart of forgiveness and a willingness to understand their perspective. **Ephesians 4:31-32 (AMP)** advises, *"Let all bitterness and wrath and anger and clamor (perpetual animosity, resentment, strife, fault-finding) and slander be put away from you, along with every kind of malice (all spitefulness, verbal abuse, malevolence). Be kind and helpful to one another, tender-hearted (compassionate, understanding), forgiving one another [readily and freely], just as God in Christ also forgave you."*

James 1:19-20 (AMP) provides valuable wisdom on handling conflicts: *"Understand this, my beloved brothers and sisters. Let everyone be quick to hear [be a careful, thoughtful listener], slow to speak [a speaker of carefully chosen words], and slow to anger; for the [resentful, deep-seated] anger of man does not produce the righteousness of God [that standard of behavior which He requires from us]."* This passage emphasizes the importance of being a good listener, controlling our speech, and managing our anger to resolve conflicts effectively.

Consider the story of Abigail and David in 1 Samuel 25. When Abigail's husband, Nabal, insulted David, David was ready to take vengeance. However, Abigail intervened with wisdom and humility, preventing a violent conflict. She approached David with respect, acknowledged the wrong, and offered a peaceful solution. David recognized her wisdom and blessed her for her actions. This story illustrates the power of a humble and wise approach in diffusing conflicts and promoting peace.

Practical Steps:

- **Pray for Guidance:** Before addressing a conflict, take a moment to pray for wisdom, patience, and a heart of understanding. **Philippians 4:6-7 (AMP)** encourages, *"Do not be anxious or worried about anything, but in everything by prayer and petition with thanksgiving, continue to make your [specific] requests known to God. And the peace of God [that peace which reassures the heart, that peace] which transcends all understanding, [that peace which] stands guard over your hearts and your minds in Christ Jesus [is yours]."*

- **Listen Actively:** Focus on truly understanding your partner's perspective. Avoid interrupting and validate their feelings. **Proverbs 18:13 (AMP)** reminds us, *"He who answers before he hears [the facts]—It is folly and shame to him."*

- **Speak the Truth in Love:** Address the issue honestly but with kindness and empathy. Avoid blame and focus on finding a resolution. **Ephesians 4:15 (AMP)** says, *"But speaking the truth in love [in all things—both our speech and our lives expressing His truth], let us grow up in all things into Him [following His example] who is the Head—Christ."*

- **Seek Forgiveness and Reconciliation:** Be willing to forgive and seek reconciliation. Holding onto grudges only harms the relationship. **Colossians 3:13 (AMP)** advises, *"Be gentle and forbearing with one another and, if one has a difference (a grievance or complaint) against another, readily pardoning each other; even as the Lord has [freely] forgiven you, so must you also [forgive]."*

- **Agree on a Plan for Future Conflicts:** Discuss and agree on how you will handle conflicts in the future. This proactive approach can help prevent misunderstandings and promote a peaceful relationship. **Amos 3:3 (AMP)** states, *"Do two walk together except they make an appointment and have agreed?"*

Spiritual Reflection:

Reflect on how you handle conflicts in your relationship. Are there areas where you need to improve in listening, patience, or forgiveness? Pray for God's guidance and strength to resolve conflicts in a Christ-like manner, and meditate on scriptures that emphasize the importance of peace and reconciliation.

Closing Thought:

Resolving conflicts in a Christ-like manner is vital for building a strong, God-centered relationship. As you and your partner commit to addressing disagreements with grace, understanding, and a heart of forgiveness, you will foster a deeper sense of trust, respect, and unity. Remember, conflict resolution is not about winning but about growing together in love and understanding.

Know Your Position in the Relationship

Embracing Your Role and Responsibilities in Love:

Understanding and embracing your position in a relationship is essential for creating a harmonious and balanced partnership. **Ephesians 5:25 (AMP)** states, *"Husbands, love your wives, seek the highest good for her and surround her with a caring, unselfish love, just as Christ also loved the church and gave Himself up for her."* This highlights the importance of sacrificial love and the roles within a relationship, urging partners to support, respect, and uplift each other.

Knowing your position involves recognizing your strengths and weaknesses and how they complement those of your partner. It requires a willingness to serve and support each other selflessly, mirroring Christ's love for the church. This understanding fosters a deep sense of respect, trust, and commitment, essential for a thriving relationship.

In practice, this means acknowledging and valuing each other's contributions, whether emotional support, financial stability, or spiritual guidance. It involves open communication about expectations and responsibilities, ensuring that both partners feel valued and understood. By embracing your role in the relationship, you create a strong foundation built on mutual respect and love.

A man's role as the head of the home is a divine responsibility that calls for leadership, love, and protection. As the head, a husband should lead with integrity, humility, and a servant's heart. He must be the pillar that provides stability and strength to his family, ensuring that his actions and decisions align with God's will. It is important for a husband to honor and cherish his wife, understanding that she is a crucial part of his life and well-being. He should never neglect her or cause her pain, as she is a bone of his bone, a vital part of his own body. Just as he would care for his own body, he should care for his wife with the same tenderness and concern (Ephesians 5:28-29).

The wife, on the other hand, is called to be a builder in her home. **Proverbs 14:1 (AMP)** says, *"The wise woman builds her house [on a foundation of godly precepts, and her household thrives], but the foolish one [who lacks spiritual insight] tears it down with her own hands [by ignoring godly principles]."* She nurtures her domain with love, prayer, and diligent effort. Her responsibility extends beyond physical tasks to spiritual nurturing, ensuring that her home is a place of peace and godliness. The wife should submit to her husband, respecting and honoring his role as the head, while also recognizing her own significant influence and responsibility in the home. She is the heart of the home, the prayer warrior, and the nurturer who builds up her children in the way of the Lord.

1 Corinthians 13:4-7 (AMP) provides a profound description of love: *"Love endures with patience and serenity, love is kind and thoughtful, and is not jealous or envious; love does not brag and is not proud or arrogant. It is not rude; it is not self-seeking, it is not provoked [nor overly sensitive and easily angered]; it does not take into account a wrong endured. It does not rejoice at injustice, but rejoices with the truth [when right and truth prevail]. Love bears all things [regardless of what comes], believes all things [looking for the best in each one], hopes all things [remaining steadfast during difficult times], endures all things [without weakening]."*

This passage calls us to exhibit patience, kindness, humility, and perseverance in our relationships. Understanding your position means applying these attributes daily, striving to love your partner as described in Scripture. For example, patience helps you navigate challenges without frustration, kindness fosters a nurturing environment, and humility allows you to prioritize your partner's needs over your own.

Consider the relationship between Ruth and Boaz in the book of Ruth. Boaz, understanding his position as a kinsman-redeemer, took responsibility to protect and providing for Ruth, demonstrating respect and love. Ruth, in turn, showed loyalty, humility, and trust in Boaz's leadership. Their story exemplifies how understanding and embracing one's role can lead to a blessed and fruitful relationship.

Practical Steps:

- **Reflect on Your Strengths and Weaknesses:** Take time to understand your abilities and limitations. Communicate these with your partner to ensure mutual understanding and support. **Romans 12:4-5 (AMP)** states, *"For just as in one [physical] body we have many parts, and these parts do not all have the same function or special use, so we, who are many, are [nevertheless just] one body in Christ, and individually [we are] parts one of another [mutually dependent on each other]."*
- **Serve Each Other Selflessly:** Embrace a servant-hearted attitude in your relationship, seeking ways to support and uplift your partner. **Mark 10:45 (AMP)** says, *"For even the Son of Man did not come to be served, but to serve, and to give His life as a ransom for many."*

- **Communicate Openly About Roles and Expectations:** Have honest discussions about each partner's responsibilities and expectations. This fosters mutual respect and ensures both partners feel valued. **Amos 3:3 (AMP)** reminds us, *"Do two walk together except they make an appointment and have agreed?"*
- **Support Each Other's Growth:** Encourage and support each other's personal and spiritual growth. Celebrate achievements and provide comfort during challenges. **Hebrews 10:24-25 (AMP)** advises, *"And let us consider [thoughtfully] how we may encourage one another to love and to do good deeds, not forsaking our meeting together [as believers for worship and instruction], as is the habit of some, but encouraging one another; and all the more [faithfully] as you see the day [of Christ's return] approaching."*
- **Pray Together:** Make prayer a regular part of your relationship, seeking God's guidance and wisdom in fulfilling your roles. **Matthew 18:20 (AMP)** says, *"For where two or three are gathered in My name [meeting together as My followers], I am there among them."*

Spiritual Reflection:

Reflect on how well you understand and embrace your role in your relationship. Are there areas where you need to grow in patience, kindness, or humility? Pray for God's guidance to fulfill your role with love and commitment, and meditate on scriptures that emphasize the importance of sacrificial love and service.

Closing Thought:

Embracing your position in a relationship is crucial for building a strong, God-centered partnership. By recognizing and fulfilling your role with love, humility, and respect, you create a harmonious and supportive environment where both partners can thrive and grow together. Remember, your role is not just a duty but a divine calling to love and serve your partner as Christ loves the church.

Encourage, Edify, and Build Up Each Other

Strengthening Each Other in Love and Faith:

Building a relationship where both partners encourage, edify, and build each other up is vital for a healthy and thriving partnership. **1 Thessalonians 5:11 (AMP)** states, *"Therefore encourage and comfort one another and build up one another, just as you are doing."* This directive emphasizes the importance of mutual support and positive reinforcement within a relationship.

Encouragement involves recognizing and affirming each other's strengths and achievements. It means being a constant source of motivation and support, especially during challenging times. When partners edify one another, they actively seek to enhance each other's spiritual, emotional, and personal growth. Building each other up entails fostering a nurturing environment where love, respect, and trust can flourish. This practice not only strengthens the relationship but also aligns it with God's purpose, making it a reflection of His love and grace.

Practically, this can be done through words of affirmation, acts of kindness, and sincere appreciation. Simple gestures like expressing gratitude, celebrating milestones, and offering a listening ear can make a significant difference. In a spiritually-driven partnership, encouraging one another also means praying together, sharing insights from Scripture, and supporting each other's spiritual journey.

Hebrews 10:24-25 (AMP) urges us to, *"And let us consider [thoughtfully] how we may encourage one another to love and to do good deeds, not forsaking our meeting together [as believers for worship and instruction], as is the habit of some, but encouraging one another; and all the more [faithfully] as you see the day [of*

Christ's return] approaching." This passage highlights the importance of intentional efforts to inspire and motivate each other toward love and good deeds.

A biblical example of encouragement is seen in the relationship between Jonathan and David. Despite the threat to his own position as the heir to the throne, Jonathan encouraged David and strengthened him in his faith. **1 Samuel 23:16 (AMP)** tells us, *"And Jonathan, Saul's son, arose and went into the woods to David [at Horesh] and encouraged him in God."* Jonathan's actions exemplify selfless support and the importance of spiritual encouragement in a relationship.

To engage readers spiritually and mentally, consider the profound impact of encouragement in your own life. Reflect on moments when someone's words or actions uplifted your spirit and motivated you to persevere. In a partnership, being a source of encouragement means consistently reminding each other of God's promises and faithfulness. It involves cultivating an environment where both partners feel valued, understood, and inspired to become the best versions of themselves.

Practical Steps:
- **Practice Active Listening:** Make a habit of truly listening to your partner. Show empathy and understanding, and offer words of comfort and encouragement. **James 1:19 (AMP)** advises, *"Understand this, my beloved brothers and sisters. Let everyone be quick to hear [be a careful, thoughtful listener], slow to speak [a speaker of carefully chosen words], and slow to anger [patient, reflective, forgiving]."*

- **Celebrate Successes and Milestones:** Acknowledge and celebrate each other's achievements, no matter how small. This fosters a sense of accomplishment and appreciation. **Romans 12:15 (AMP)** encourages us to, *"Rejoice with those who rejoice [sharing others' joy], and weep with those who weep [sharing others' grief]."*

- **Offer Constructive Feedback:** When providing feedback, do so with love and a focus on growth. Avoid criticism that tears down, and instead, offer insights that build up. **Ephesians 4:29 (AMP)** says, *"Do not let unwholesome [foul, profane, worthless, vulgar] words ever come out of your mouth, but only such speech as is good for building up others, according to the need and the occasion, so that it will be a blessing to those who hear [you speak]."*

- **Pray Together:** Make prayer a regular practice in your relationship. Pray for each other's needs, dreams, and spiritual growth. **Matthew 18:20 (AMP)** states, *"For where two or three are gathered in My name [meeting together as My followers], I am there among them."*

- **Share Scripture and Spiritual Insights:** Regularly share meaningful Bible verses and insights that can inspire and uplift your partner. This reinforces a shared spiritual foundation and encourages mutual growth. **Colossians 3:16 (AMP)** urges us to, *"Let the [spoken] word of Christ have its home within you [dwelling in your heart and mind—permeating every aspect of your being] as you teach [spiritual things] and admonish and train one another with all wisdom, singing psalms and hymns and spiritual songs with thankfulness in your hearts to God."*

Spiritual Reflection:

Take a moment to reflect on how you can be a source of encouragement to your partner. Consider the ways in which you can offer support, understanding, and motivation. Pray for the wisdom to speak words that build up and for the grace to create an environment of mutual edification and love.

Closing Thought:

Encouraging, edifying, and building up each other are vital components of a Christ-centered relationship. By practicing these principles, you not only strengthen your partnership but also create a reflection of God's love and grace in your lives. Remember, your words and actions have the power to inspire, uplift, and transform, making your relationship a beacon of hope and faith.

Pursue Holiness and Sexual Purity

Embracing Purity and Holiness in Your Relationship:

In a world where moral standards often shift, maintaining sexual purity and pursuing holiness in a relationship can be challenging but immensely rewarding. **1 Thessalonians 4:3-4 (AMP)** teaches, *"For this is the will of God, that you be sanctified [separated and set apart from sin]: that you abstain from sexual immorality; that each of you knows how to control his own body in holiness and honor."* This passage underscores the importance of honoring God through our physical bodies and maintaining sexual purity as a testament to our commitment to His will.

Remaining pure until marriage involves setting clear standards, boundaries, and expectations within the relationship. This commitment not only honors God but also strengthens the emotional and spiritual bond between partners. Establishing standards means agreeing on what is acceptable behavior within the relationship and ensuring these align with biblical principles. Boundaries help protect the relationship from temptations and keep both partners accountable. Expectations involve clear communication about the desires and goals for the relationship, ensuring both partners are on the same page and working towards a shared vision.

Moreover, pursuing holiness means striving for a lifestyle that reflects God's character and principles. It involves daily choices that align with God's Word, fostering a heart and mind that seeks to honor Him in all aspects of life. This commitment to holiness and purity lays a strong foundation for a lasting and fulfilling relationship, where both partners grow closer to each other and to God.

Proverbs 4:23 (AMP) advises, *"Watch over your heart with all diligence, for from it flow the springs of life."* This verse highlights the importance of guarding our hearts and minds against influences that can lead us away from God's path. It reminds us that our thoughts and desires shape our actions and ultimately determine the direction of our lives.

A biblical example of purity and integrity can be seen in the story of Joseph. Despite being tempted by Potiphar's wife, Joseph chose to flee from sin, declaring, *"How then could I do this great evil and sin against God?"* **(Genesis 39:9, AMP)**. His unwavering commitment to purity and holiness, even in the face of severe temptation, demonstrates the importance of upholding God's standards and trusting in His plan.

To engage readers spiritually and mentally, consider the profound impact of purity and holiness in your relationship. Reflect on how a commitment to these principles can transform your partnership, bringing you closer to each other and to God. Meditate on the ways in which maintaining sexual purity and pursuing holiness can lead to a deeper, more fulfilling connection rooted in God's love and grace.

Practical Steps:

- **Set Clear Boundaries:** Discuss and establish clear boundaries regarding physical intimacy. Agree on activities that honor your commitment to purity and support each other in upholding these standards. **1 Corinthians 6:18 (AMP)** instructs, *"Run away from sexual immorality [in any form, whether thought or behavior, whether visual or written]. Every other sin that a man commits is outside the body, but the one who is sexually immoral sins against his own body."*

- **Engage in Spiritual Activities Together:** Strengthen your bond by engaging in spiritual activities such as prayer, Bible study, and worship. These practices foster a deeper connection with God and reinforce your commitment to purity. **Matthew 5:8 (AMP)** states, *"Blessed [anticipating God's presence, spiritually mature] are the pure in heart [those with integrity, moral courage, and godly character], for they will see God."*

- **Seek Accountability:** Surround yourselves with a community of believers who can offer support and hold you accountable in your pursuit of purity and holiness. **Proverbs 27:17 (AMP)** says, *"As iron sharpens iron, so one man sharpens [and influences] another [through discussion]."*

- **Guard Your Heart and Mind:** Be mindful of the content you consume and the influences you allow into your relationship. Choose activities and entertainment that align with your values and reinforce your commitment to purity. **Philippians 4:8 (AMP)** encourages, *"Finally, believers, whatever is true, whatever is honorable and worthy of respect, whatever is right and confirmed by God's word, whatever is pure and wholesome, whatever is lovely and brings peace, whatever is admirable and of good repute; if there is any excellence, if there is anything worthy of praise, think continually on these things [center your mind on them, and implant them in your heart]."*

- **Pray for Strength and Guidance:** Regularly seek God's guidance and strength to uphold your commitment to purity and holiness. Trust in His provision and rely on His grace to navigate challenges. **Psalm 51:10 (AMP)** pleads, *"Create in me a clean heart, O God, and renew a right and steadfast spirit within me."*

Spiritual Reflection:

Take a moment to reflect on the significance of pursuing holiness and maintaining sexual purity in your relationship. Consider how these commitments can shape your partnership and bring you closer to God's purpose for your lives. Pray for the wisdom, strength, and courage to uphold these values and to honor God in all aspects of your relationship.

Closing Thought:

Pursuing holiness and maintaining sexual purity are vital components of a God-centered relationship. By committing to these principles, you not only honor God but also build a strong, lasting foundation for your partnership. Remember, your dedication to purity and holiness is a testament to your faith and a reflection of God's love and grace in your lives.

CONCLUSION

Embracing God's Blueprint for Relationships

Embarking on the journey to prepare for your purpose partner through these 12 steps is a profound and transformative process. Each step, rooted in biblical principles, guides you to develop a relationship that honors God and aligns with His divine will. By prioritizing a personal relationship with God, understanding His vision for your life, cultivating godly character, and practicing self-control, you lay a strong foundation for a thriving partnership. Submitting to God's will, establishing financial responsibility, and mastering effective communication further reinforce this foundation, ensuring a resilient and harmonious relationship.

As you grow personally and hold each other accountable, resolving conflicts in a Christ-like manner and knowing your roles within the relationship become pivotal. Encouraging, edifying, and building up each other fosters a supportive environment where both partners can flourish. Pursuing holiness and maintaining sexual purity safeguard the sanctity of your relationship, while setting standards, boundaries, and expectations, and guarding your heart and mind to fortify your commitment to God's principles.

In a world where relationships often face numerous challenges, adhering to these steps enables you to build a partnership that stands the test of time. It's not just about finding a partner; it's about becoming the right partner—one who reflects Christ's love, exhibits godly character, and is committed to a shared vision rooted in faith.

Incorporating Dr. Myles Munroe's Insights:

In choosing a spouse, you must possess and check out for the presence of these eight traits: adaptability, empathy, ability to work through problems, ability to give and receive love, emotional stability, ability to communicate, similarities between the couples themselves, and similar family background. These traits significantly increase the chances of a successful and harmonious relationship.

- **Adaptability:** Adaptability is crucial in a relationship because it emphasizes adjusting to each other despite differences. This trait ensures that differences don't become obstacles but opportunities for growth and understanding.
- **Empathy:** Empathy is essential as it involves sensitivity to each other's needs, hurts, and desires. A marriage thrives when both partners are attuned to each other's emotional states and willing to meet those needs.
- **Ability to Work Through Problems:** A successful marriage consists of partners committed to solving problems together and finding ways around challenges. Ignoring issues only leads to dissatisfaction and unresolved conflict.
- **Ability to Give and Receive Love:** Love must flow both ways in a marriage. Both partners must be willing to express love and be open to receiving it, ensuring a balanced and nurturing relationship.
- **Emotional Stability:** Emotional stability involves controlling emotions and avoiding immature outbursts. It's about harnessing the will to manage emotions constructively.
- **Ability to Communicate:** Effective communication is the bedrock of any relationship. Couples must understand and express their intentions and feelings clearly, recognizing that men and women often communicate differently.

- **Similarities Between the Couples Themselves:** While differences exist, having common interests, hobbies, faith, or political views provides a shared foundation that strengthens the relationship.
- **Similar Family Background:** Couples with similar family backgrounds may find it easier to adapt to each other, reducing potential conflicts and misunderstandings. Now, people with different backgrounds can have successful marriages but these traits are focusing on increasing the chances. People with similar family backgrounds will find it easier to get along with each other because there will be fewer things to adapt to.

Proverbs 18:22 (AMP) tells us, *"He who finds a [true and faithful] wife finds a good thing and obtains favor and approval from the Lord."* This verse underscores the blessing that comes with a godly marriage, highlighting the importance of choosing a partner who aligns with God's principles and purpose.

As you reflect on these steps, consider how each one contributes to a relationship that not only brings joy and fulfillment but also honors God. In **Ephesians 5:25-27 (AMP),** Paul instructs husbands to love their wives *"just as Christ also loved the church and gave Himself up for her, so that He might sanctify the church, having cleansed her by the washing of water with the word [of God], so that [in turn] He might present the church to Himself in glorious splendor, without spot or wrinkle or any such thing; but that she would be holy [set apart for God] and blameless."*

Spiritual Reflection:

Take time to meditate on these scriptures and the journey you have undertaken through these 12 steps. Pray for continued guidance, strength, and wisdom as you apply these principles to your relationship. Remember that the journey doesn't end here; it's a continuous process of growth, learning, and deepening your faith.

Reflect on how each step has shaped your perspective on relationships and your role as a partner. Consider the ways you can continue to grow individually and together, always striving to align your relationship with God's will. Trust in His timing and His plan, knowing that as you commit to these principles, you are building a relationship that honors Him and is blessed by His favor. Continue to seek His wisdom, apply these steps diligently, and watch as your relationship flourishes under His guidance and grace.

Made in the USA
Middletown, DE
07 February 2025